Alaska

Xavier W. Niz

Consultant:
Jeanner Eder, Ph.D.
Director of Alaska Native Studies
and Associate Professor of History
University of Alaska-Anchorage
Anchorage, Alaska

Capstone
press
Mankato, Minnesota

Capstone Press
151 Good Counsel Drive • P.O. Box 669 • Mankato, Minnesota 56002
http://www.capstone-press.com

Library of Congress Cataloging-in-Publication Data
Niz, Xavier.
    Alaska / Xavier W. Niz.
    v. cm.—(Land of liberty)
    Includes bibliographical references and index.
    Contents: About Alaska—Land, climate, and wildlife—History of Alaska—
Government and politics—Economy and resources—People and culture.
    ISBN 0-7368-1570-8 (hardcover)
    1. Alaska—Juvenile literature. [1. Alaska.] I. Title. II. Series.
F904.3 .N59 2003
979.8—dc21   2002013993

Summary: An introduction to the geography, history, government, politics, economy,
resources, people, and culture of Alaska, including maps, charts, and a recipe.

Editorial Credits
Blake A. Hoena, editor; Jennifer Schonborn, series designer; Linda Clavel, book
    designer; Angi Gahler, illustrator; Kelly Garvin, photo researcher; Eric
    Kudalis, product planning editor

Photo Credits
Cover images: moose in Denali National Park and Preserve, Robin Brandt; fishing
boat in Whaler's Cove near Admiralty Island, Kent & Donna Dannen

Alaska Division of Tourism/Earnst Schneider, 42; Alaska Division of
Tourism/Robert Angell, 15; Alaska State Library, 35; Capstone Press/Gary
Sundermeyer, 54; Corbis/Bettmann, 22, 25, 36; Corbis/Danny Lehman, 41;
Corbis/Douglas Peebles, 44; Corbis/Gunter Marx Photography, 23; Corbis/Jack
Fields, 12–13; Corbis/Kennan Ward, 14; Corbis/Kevin Fleming, 38–39;
Corbis/Paul A. Soulders, 4; Corbis/Pat O'Hara, 28–29; Corbis/Vince Streano, 50;
Craig Brandt, 8; Houserstock/Dave G. Houser, 30; Hulton Archive by Getty
Images, 16, 20, 58; Kent & Donna Dannen, 48–49; North Wind Picture Archives,
19; One Mile Up, Inc., 55 (both); Robert McCaw, 56, 57; Robin Brandt, 27, 53,
63; Wolfgang Kaehler/www.wkaehlerphoto.com, 43;
U.S. Postal Service, 59

Design Elements
Autograph Series, Digital Stock, PhotoDisc, Inc.

1 2 3 4 5 6 08 07 06 05 04 03

Table of Contents

During the Iditarod, mushers race teams
of sled dogs from Anchorage to Nome.

Chapter 1

About Alaska

On the first Saturday in March, the Iditarod Trail Sled Dog Race begins. Dogsled drivers race teams of sled dogs across Alaska's winter landscape. Mushers cross mountains and race over frozen lakes. Because of the Iditarod's challenges, people often say it is "the last great race on Earth." People from all over the world come to watch and take part in the race.

People used the Iditarod Trail in the late 1800s and early 1900s. They carried mail and supplies from Seward to settlers and gold miners in western Alaska. Few roads existed at the time. Dogsleds were the easiest way to carry items from place to place in winter.

In 1925, a diphtheria outbreak occurred in Nome. Doctors sent medicine from Anchorage to help those who were sick. The medicine could be shipped only part way by train. Mushers carried it the rest of the way on the Iditarod Trail. The medicine saved hundreds of lives.

The first Anchorage-to-Nome sled dog race was held in 1973. This race honored the historic dogsled run of 1925. Since 1973, the Iditarod has been run every year. The race covers more than 1,000 miles (1,600 kilometers).

The Last Frontier State

People call Alaska the Last Frontier State. Most of Alaska is undeveloped wilderness. Mountains, glaciers, forests, tundra, and active volcanoes cover the state.

Alaska is the largest state. It is more than twice the area of Texas, which is the second largest state. Yet, Alaska is one of the least populated states. Fewer than 700,000 people live there.

Alaska is not connected to the lower 48 states. Canada's British Columbia and Yukon Territory border Alaska to the east. The Arctic Ocean is north of Alaska. The Pacific Ocean

Alaska Cities

ARCTIC OCEAN

RUSSIA

Bering Strait

• Barrow

Prudhoe • Bay

• Nome

Fairbanks •

ALASKA

Bering Sea

NORTHWEST TERRITORIES

CANADA

YUKON TERRITORY

Anchorage • • Valdez

Seward •

BRITISH COLUMBIA

Legend

⊛ Capital

• City

• Kodiak

Kodiak Island

⊛ Juneau

Sitka •

Ketchikan •

N

W   E

S

Scale
Miles
0   100   200   300   400   500

0   100 200 300 400 500
Kilometers

PACIFIC OCEAN

lies to its south. To the west, the Bering Sea and the Bering
Strait separate Alaska from Russia.

Mount McKinley is the highest mountain in North America. Alaskan Natives call this mountain Denali.

Chapter 2

Land, Climate, and Wildlife

Alaska can be divided into five land regions. These areas
are the Panhandle, the Southcentral, the Alaska Peninsula, the
Interior, and the Arctic.

The Land

The Panhandle includes islands, inlets, and peninsulas. This
narrow strip of land lies between British Columbia, Canada
and the Gulf of Alaska. The Panhandle is covered by mountains
and forests. The Malaspina Glacier lies in the northern part of
the Panhandle. This sheet of ice covers an area larger than the
state of Rhode Island.

The Southcentral stretches from the Malaspina Glacier west to the Alaska Peninsula. This area is covered with glaciers, mountains, forests, lakes, and rivers. The Southcentral also includes the Alaska Range. Mount McKinley is within this group of mountains. The south peak of Mount McKinley rises 20,320 feet (6,194 meters) above sea level. It is the highest point in North America.

In southwestern Alaska, the Alaska Peninsula extends into the Pacific Ocean. This region also includes the Aleutian Islands and Kodiak Island. The Aleutian Range runs through the Alaska Peninsula and the Aleutian Islands. Many active volcanoes are in this mountain range.

The Interior lies between the Alaska Range to the south and the Brooks Range to the north. Several small mountain ranges spread across the area. They give the land a rolling appearance. The Interior includes the Yukon Flats, which is a large area of swampy land called muskeg.

The Arctic runs from the Brooks Range north to the Arctic Ocean. This area also is known as the North Slope. The Arctic includes flat, mostly treeless plains called tundra. Beneath the tundra is permafrost, frozen soil that does not thaw.

Alaska's Land Features

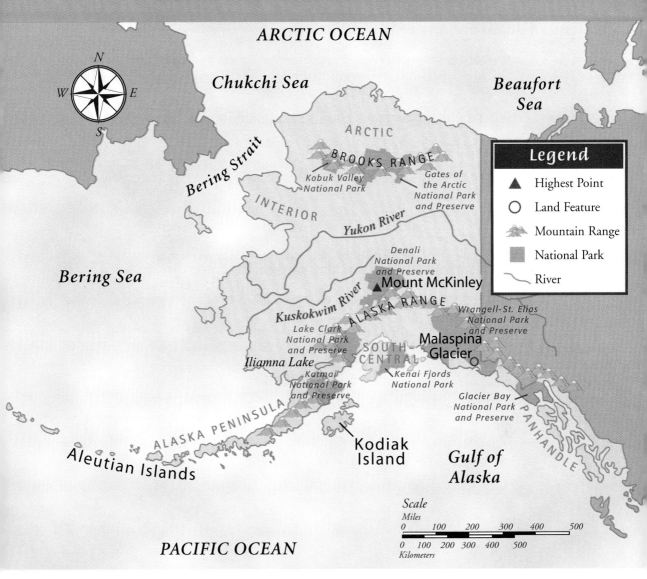

Map legend:

Legend
- ▲ Highest Point
- ○ Land Feature
- 🞄 Mountain Range
- ▪ National Park
- 〜 River

Map labels:

ARCTIC OCEAN

Chukchi Sea

Beaufort Sea

Bering Strait

Bering Sea

ARCTIC

BROOKS RANGE

Kobuk Valley National Park

Gates of the Arctic National Park and Preserve

INTERIOR

Yukon River

Denali National Park and Preserve

▲ Mount McKinley

Kuskokwim River

ALASKA RANGE

Wrangell-St. Elias National Park and Preserve

Lake Clark National Park and Preserve

Iliamna Lake

SOUTH-CENTRAL

Malaspina Glacier ○

Katmai National Park and Preserve

Kenai Fjords National Park

Glacier Bay National Park and Preserve

PANHANDLE

ALASKA PENINSULA

Aleutian Islands

Kodiak Island

Gulf of Alaska

PACIFIC OCEAN

Scale
Miles
0   100   200   300   400   500
0 100 200 300 400 500
Kilometers

Rivers and Lakes

Alaska has about 3,000 rivers. The Yukon River is the longest.
It is 1,980 miles (3,190 kilometers) long. This river starts in

Canada and flows through Alaska to the Bering Sea. Alaska's second longest river is the Kuskokwim River. It flows for 724 miles (1,165 kilometers).

Alaska has more than 3 million lakes. Iliamna Lake is the state's largest lake. It lies at the foot of the Alaska Peninsula. This lake covers 1,033 square miles (2,675 square kilometers).

Climate

Alaska's climate varies from area to area. Warm air from the sea gives coastal areas a mild climate. Maritime temperatures

do not get very hot or very cold. The Interior has the state's coldest and hottest temperatures. Temperatures can range from 100 degrees Fahrenheit (38 degrees Celsius) in summer to minus 80 degrees Fahrenheit (minus 62 degrees Celsius) in winter.

Rainfall and snowfall also vary from area to area. The Panhandle gets a great deal of rain. The Interior is covered in snow during winter. The Alaska Peninsula is the wettest region of the state. It may receive more than 200 inches (508 centimeters) of precipitation each year.

The Yukon River flows across Alaska to the Bering Sea.

Plant Life and Wildlife

Plant life thrives in Alaska. Large forests of Sitka spruce, western hemlock, canoe cedar, and Alaska cedar trees grow in the Panhandle. The Southcentral is covered with Sitka spruce, white cedar, and black cedar trees. Many wildflowers grow on the Alaska Peninsula and in the Interior. Lichens, mosses, and shrubs cover the Arctic.

Many large animals live in Alaska. Black bears, brown bears, and polar bears are common. Kodiak bears are a type of brown bear found on Kodiak Island. They are the largest meat-eating mammals that live on land. Musk oxen, caribou, moose, elk, and reindeer are other large animals that live in Alaska.

Killer whales, also known as orcas, swim in Alaska's coastal waters.

Polar Bears

Polar bears are one of the largest animals found in Alaska. They weigh up to 1,500 pounds (680 kilograms). Their range includes the northern and the northwestern coasts of Alaska.

Polar bears are known for their white fur. But the fur actually is clear. Sunlight reflecting off the fur makes it look white. The white coloring helps polar bears blend in with ice and snow, making it difficult for prey animals to see them.

Polar bears are good swimmers. They have been seen swimming as far as 50 miles (80 kilometers) from shore. Their fur is oily and repels water. These qualities keep polar bears warm while swimming in cold arctic waters.

Alaska's shores and coastal waters are filled with sea life. Many types of fish live there. Dolphins, sea otters, seals, and sea lions are common. Killer whales, sperm whales, and gray whales swim off Alaska's coasts.

Many types of birds live in Alaska. Ducks, geese, swans, cranes, loons, and gulls can be found on Alaska's lakes. Golden eagles, peregrine falcons, and bald eagles make Alaska their home. Alaska has more bald eagles than any other state.

Aleuts have lived in Alaska for thousands of years. They settled the Aleutian Islands in western Alaska.

Chapter 3

History of Alaska

Around 50,000 years ago, Earth's surface looked very different. Land now covered with water was dry then. Scientists believe people called Paleo-Indians crossed the Bering Land Bridge during this time. The Bering Land Bridge was a stretch of land that once connected Asia to North America. People are not sure which way the Paleo-Indians traveled. Some scientists believe they may have crossed from Asia to North America. These scientists believe Paleo-Indians were the first people to come to Alaska and North America.

Some of Alaska's early people formed three main cultures. These Alaskan Natives are Eskimos, Aleuts, and Athabascans. Eskimos lived along Alaska's coastal regions. Aleuts were

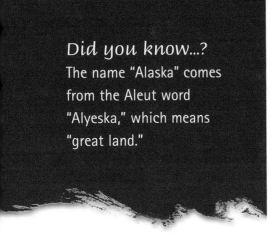

sea travelers who settled on the Aleutian Islands. Athabascans were hunters who roamed throughout the Interior.

Exploration of Alaska

In the early 1700s, Russian ruler Peter the Great wondered if Asia and North America were joined. He sent Vitus Bering, a Danish sailor who worked for the Russian Navy, to find out. In 1728, Bering sailed north through what is now called the Bering Strait. He found that this waterway separates Asia and North America.

In June 1741, Bering set out on a second trip. He wanted to reach North America. In July, Bering reached Alaska. He gathered animal furs, plants, and birds to take back to Russia. Bering became ill and died during the return trip to Russia. But the sea otter, blue fox, and seal furs his crew brought back sparked the interest of Russian fur traders.

The fur trade made money for Russia, but it was damaging to Alaskan Natives. Many Alaskan Natives died from smallpox, measles, pneumonia, and other European diseases. The Russians enslaved and killed many Aleuts.

By 1800, Alaska's Aleut population had dropped from about 25,000 to fewer than 2,500.

The U.S. Purchase of Alaska

In the mid-1800s, Russian leaders were losing interest in their American colony. The fur trade was not doing well. Fur traders had killed many sea otters and seals, and these animals were becoming difficult to find.

The United States was interested in Alaska. Alaska had large fish populations along its coasts. Alaska also had deposits

Vitus Bering's ship was destroyed on his voyage back to Russia. Bering died of an illness while shipwrecked.

of copper, coal, and gold. U.S. Secretary of State William Seward began talking to Russian leaders. The United States was interested in buying Russia's American territories.

In 1867, the United States bought Russia's claim to Alaska for $7.2 million, or 2 cents an acre (5 cents per hectare). But not all Americans were happy with this purchase. Some people thought it was foolish to spend money on an area that they believed was a frozen wasteland. They called Alaska "Seward's Folly" or "Seward's Icebox."

In the late 1800s, gold attracted many people to Alaska. People panned for gold in Alaska's rivers and streams.

"...it was a beautiful sight to see the large pieces of quartz, spangled over with gold."

—Robert Harris, Alaskan gold prospector

Few people took interest in the newest U.S. territory. Fewer than 35,000 people lived in Alaska in 1880. Then prospectors Joe Juneau and Richard Harris discovered gold in southeastern Alaska. Thousands of people rushed to the area. They hoped to find gold and become rich. More gold rushes soon followed as gold was found in other parts of Alaska. People began to realize Alaska's value. By 1900, the state's population had risen to more than 60,000.

The Road to Statehood

Gold was only one of Alaska's many riches. Coal was discovered at Cook Inlet. Copper mines opened in Kennecott. Salmon fisheries were built along the southern coast. Lumber companies logged Alaska's large forests.

Alaska's many industries brought more people to the territory. As Alaska developed, its residents hoped for statehood. As a U.S. territory, Alaskans were not able to vote for the U.S. president or elect their own governor.

In the early 1900s, Congress tried to pass several bills to make Alaska a state. Each bill failed.

During the Great Depression (1929–1939), the country's economy suffered. Many businesses closed, and workers lost their jobs. But Alaska's abundant natural resources helped its industries grow during this time. Many people moved to Alaska to find work. As the population grew, people made louder demands to make Alaska a state.

During World War II (1939–1945), U.S. leaders were worried about Alaska. Alaska's westernmost islands lay close to

During World War II, U.S. Army workers built a highway to connect Alaska to the lower 48 states.

This stretch of the Alaska Highway runs along the Racing River in British Columbia, Canada.

the enemy nation of Japan. The U.S. military quickly moved troops to the area.

Before the war, Alaska could be reached only by ship or airplane. The U.S. Army Corps of Engineers built the Alaska-Canada Military Highway from Dawson, British Columbia, to Fairbanks, Alaska. This 1,520-mile (2,446-kilometer) road took eight months to build. It helped link Alaska to the lower 48 states.

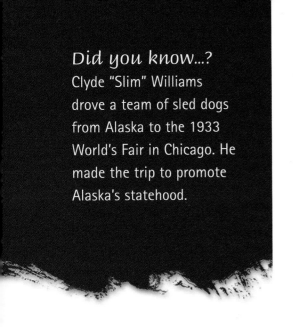

On June 3, 1942, Japanese soldiers attacked the U.S. Navy base in the Aleutian Islands. A few days later, Japanese soldiers captured the islands of Attu and Kiska. The United States did not win back these islands until the end of August 1943.

After the war, many military and civilian workers decided to stay and live in Alaska. The sudden growth in population again increased demands for Alaska's statehood.

In 1955, delegates from Alaska met in Fairbanks. After 73 days, these people created the Alaska state constitution. Alaskans hoped their constitution would prove that Alaska was ready for statehood.

On January 3, 1959, President Dwight Eisenhower signed a bill making Alaska the 49th state. Juneau became the state capital. William Egan was elected Alaska's first state governor.

Alaska Today

The new state quickly suffered two natural disasters. In March 1964, an earthquake shook the Anchorage area. It was the most powerful earthquake ever recorded in North America.

More than 100 people died. Damage from the earthquake cost more than $400 million. In 1967, Fairbanks experienced the worst flood in its history. Five people died. More than $84 million in damages were reported.

In 1968, Alaska's future brightened. Large oil deposits were found at Prudhoe Bay. A pipeline was built across Alaska to transport the oil to the southern port city of Valdez. Many people moved to Alaska to build the pipeline. Alaska's population grew by almost one-third. Money from oil sales helped state and local governments build community centers,

In 1964, an earthquake damaged parts of downtown Anchorage.

schools, highways, and airstrips. Money from oil also allowed Alaska to get rid of its state income tax.

In 1971, Congress passed the Alaska Native Land Claims Act. This law gave $962.5 million and returned 44 million acres (18 million hectares) of land to Alaskan Natives. Today, several Alaskan Native groups manage this land and money. Together, these groups are one of the state's largest employers. They use the land and money to provide Alaskan Natives with an education and a job. They also help Alaskan Natives start businesses.

In 1980, Congress passed the Alaska National Interest Lands Conservation Act. This law added 104 million acres (42 million hectares) to Alaska's national park lands. The law protected the lands. Companies could no longer mine, log, or build on park lands. Environmentalists liked the new law, but not all Alaskans were happy. After the act was passed, the federal government controlled more than 60 percent of Alaska's land. Many Alaskans feel that they should be responsible for the land use in their state.

Trans-Alaska Pipeline

In 1974, the Alyeska Pipeline Service Company began work on the Trans-Alaska Pipeline. The pipeline was finished in 1977. It extends from Prudhoe Bay to Valdez.

Environmentalists and Alaskans had many worries about the pipeline. A pipeline across the Interior could keep caribou, elk, and other large animals from migrating. Oil is warm when it comes out of the ground. People worried that warm pipes would melt the permafrost, damaging wilderness areas. People also worried that a leak or an oil spill would harm wildlife.

Several design elements helped solve people's concerns. More than half of the pipeline is raised 5 to 15 feet (1.5 to 4.6 meters) off the ground. This design allows animals to travel under the pipeline. It also keeps warm pipes from melting the permafrost. The pipeline was built to zigzag across the land. This design helps prevent leaks by allowing pipes to shift during earthquakes and weather changes.

On March 24, 1989, disaster struck Alaska again. The oil tanker *Exxon Valdez* hit a reef off southern Alaska's coast. The accident spilled 11 million gallons (42 million liters) of crude oil into Prince William Sound. Wind and tides coated long stretches of coastline with oil. The spill killed countless birds, seals, and fish. Many fisheries had to close. The Exxon oil company paid billions of dollars to repair damages and to clean up the oil. But almost 15 years later, the area has not fully recovered from the spill.

Alaskan land arguments recently focused on the Arctic National Wildlife Refuge. Large oil and natural gas deposits lie beneath this area. Environmentalists, oil company officials, and government officials have talked about the dangers and the rewards of drilling for oil in the refuge. In 2002, U.S. Congress members voted against allowing oil companies to search for oil in the area. They feared that drilling for oil might harm the refuge's wildlife.

The U.S. government set up the Arctic National Wildlife Refuge in 1960. This park was created to protect wildlife in the area. Caribou, wolves, musk oxen, wolverines, snow geese, and many other animals live in the refuge.

Workers finished Alaska's state capitol building in 1931.

Chapter 4

Government and Politics

Alaska's government has greatly changed since Alaska became part of the United States in 1867. The U.S. Army controlled the area in its early years. Today, a state constitution divides Alaska's government into three branches. These branches are the executive, the legislative, and the judicial.

State Government

The executive branch carries out state laws. The governor and the lieutenant governor head Alaska's executive branch. They are elected to four-year terms. The executive branch also includes 15 state departments. These departments oversee government policies. State departments take care of education, environmental conservation, health and social services, and natural resources programs. The governor appoints many of the people who head these departments. The governor also appoints the state's judges.

Members of the legislative branch make laws for Alaska. Alaska's legislature is made of a 20-member senate and a 40-member house of representatives. Senators serve four-year terms. Representatives serve two-year terms.

Alaska's judicial branch has four levels of courts. District courts are the lowest level. They handle minor criminal and civil cases. Superior courts are above the district courts. Serious criminal and civil cases as well as appeals from district courts are heard in superior courts. The next level is the court of appeals. This court reviews criminal cases from the superior courts. The state's highest court is its supreme court. The supreme court has the final say over all lower-court rulings.

Alaska's Government

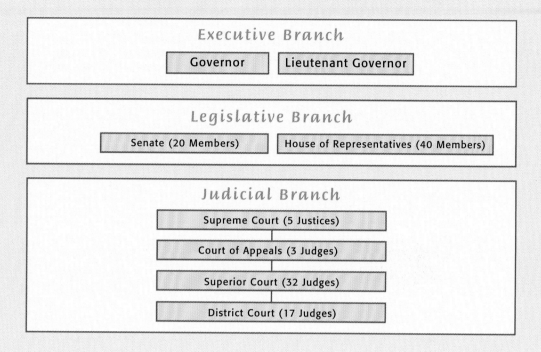

Local Government

Alaska is divided into 16 local governments called organized boroughs. Boroughs are like counties in other states. They may include cities, suburbs, and rural areas. Organized boroughs operate public schools, plan land use, and collect taxes.

"Alaskans understand better than most Americans the necessity of maintaining the health of our land."
— *Alaska Governor Tony Knowles, in a letter to members of the U.S. Senate, March 21, 2001*

An assembly of five to 11 elected members runs each borough. In most boroughs, an elected mayor oversees the assembly. In other boroughs, the assembly picks a manager to govern the borough.

More than 85 percent of Alaska's population lives in organized boroughs. But these boroughs cover only 44 percent of Alaska. The rest of the state is called an unorganized borough. This area is mostly wilderness. It is governed by the state legislature.

James Wickersham

James Wickersham was one of Alaska's most important politicians. Born in 1857, Wickersham moved to Alaska in 1900. He was a federal judge.

Wickersham helped bring justice to Alaska. He set up his first court in the settlement of Eagle. He traveled to distant settlements by boat in the summer and by dogsled in the winter.

Wickersham also served in the U.S. Congress as Alaska's nonvoting delegate. Wickersham fought for Alaska's rights. In 1914, he won approval for the Alaska Railroad from Seward to Fairbanks. He introduced the first bill for Alaska's statehood in 1916. In 1917, he helped establish Mount McKinley National Park, which is now called Denali National Park and Preserve.

After his successful career in Washington, D.C., Wickersham moved to Juneau. He died in 1939. Today, visitors can see his house in Chicken Ridge, a historic neighborhood of Juneau.

Alaska's population rapidly grew during the gold rushes of the late 1800s. People came to Alaska with hopes of finding gold and becoming rich.

Economy and Resources

The history of Alaska has been a history of its economy. From its earliest days, Alaska's resources have shaped its future. In the 1700s, Alaska's large populations of sea otters and seals attracted Russian fur traders and settlers. The area's rich mineral deposits and fish populations attracted the interest of the United States in the mid-1800s. The gold rushes of the late 1800s helped populate Alaska.

Due to its natural resources, Alaska has a "boom or bust" economy. When its resources are in demand, the state thrives. When demand drops and prices are low, the state suffers. The growth of Alaska's service industries are helping to beat this boom or bust cycle.

Alaska imports most of its food and consumer goods. This need causes high prices and a high cost of living for Alaskans. State officials are encouraging the development of Alaska's manufacturing industries. Food and consumer goods produced in state will cost Alaskans less than imported goods.

Fishing and Agriculture

Alaska's most dependable source of income comes from fishing. The state's annual seafood catch is worth almost

$3 billion. Alaska's fisheries produce more seafood than any other state in the country. Alaska's fisheries are the state's largest private employers.

Alaska has 1.4 million acres (.6 million hectares) of farmland. Crops account for two-thirds of Alaska's agricultural income. Livestock and poultry products provide the rest. Milk is Alaska's most valuable agricultural product. Alaska's farms also produce eggs, beef, hay, and potatoes. The rich soil of the Matanuska-Susitna Valley produces almost three-fourths of Alaska's farm products.

Fishing is one of Alaska's most important industries. Fishers catch salmon, pollock, cod, halibut, herring, and smelt in Alaska's waters.

"To the lover of pure wildness, Alaska is one of the most wonderful countries in the world."

—John Muir (1838–1914), nature writer

Mining and Timber

Crude oil is Alaska's main mining product. Alaska provides almost one-fourth of the oil produced in the United States. Most of Alaska's oil comes from the Prudhoe Bay area. Many people believe the state's largest oil deposits lie under the Arctic National Wildlife Refuge.

Alaska has several other important mining products. Natural gas is pumped from the Kenai Peninsula and Cook Inlet areas. Gold is mined near Fairbanks and Nome. The Red Dog Zinc Mine near Kotzebue holds the largest deposit of zinc in the United States. Other important Alaskan mining products include coal, lead, and silver.

While 24 percent of Alaska is covered in forests, only 4 million acres (1.6 million hectares) of land are valuable for logging. The Tongass National Forest in southeastern Alaska provides most of the state's lumber.

Service Industries

Alaska's many service industries add to the state's economy. Schools, hotels, entertainment, and health services are all examples of service industries. Government work is Alaska's most important service industry. More than 30 percent of working Alaskans have jobs with federal, state, or local agencies. Government services include the running of public schools, public hospitals, and military bases.

Oil platforms allow oil companies to drill for oil offshore. This platform is located in Alaska's Cook Inlet.

Tourism is another important service industry in Alaska. Each year, more than 1 million people visit Alaska. Most visit during the summer. Tourists spend more than $1.2 billion each year in Alaska. Alaska's many national parks add to the growth of tourism.

Manufacturing

Manufacturing makes up only 4 percent of Alaska's state income. Food processing is Alaska's leading manufacturing activity. This industry includes the production of canned and

The Central Gas Factory in Prudhoe Bay is the world's largest natural gas plant.

Alaska's many parks attract thousands of visitors each year.

frozen fish products. Ketchikan, Dillingham, Kodiak, and many coastal cities have factories to process fish.

Oil products result in Alaska's second largest manufacturing activity. Fairbanks, Kenai, and Prudhoe Bay have large oil refineries to process oil into gasoline.

Wood products also are important to Alaska's manufacturing industry. These goods include round logs, lumber, wood pulp, and paper products.

Each year, the Anchorage Fur Rendezvous is held in Alaska's largest city. People go to this festival for fur auctions, car races, and a costume dance.

Chapter 6

People and Culture

Alaska is the largest state, but it is one of the least populated. Fewer than 700,000 people live in Alaska. Only Vermont and Wyoming have fewer people than Alaska.

Most Alaskans live in cities located along Alaska's coasts or in river valleys. More than two-thirds of Alaskans live in urban areas. Alaska's largest city is Anchorage. More than 250,000 people, or 40 percent of all Alaskans, live in Anchorage. Other large cities include Juneau, Fairbanks, and Sitka.

Alaska has several ethnic groups. More than two-thirds of Alaskans are white. The next largest group is American Indians and Alaskan Natives. Alaska has small Asian, Hispanic, and African American populations. Almost 6 percent of Alaskans have parents with different ethnic backgrounds from each other. This percentage is twice the national average.

Education

Public schools in Alaska range from one-room schoolhouses in small villages to large high schools in cities. Some students live too far away from a village to attend a regular school. These students get their lessons and turn in their homework by mail. Today, this education program also uses satellite television and the Internet to help students in faraway areas complete their schoolwork.

Transportation

Traveling in Alaska can be difficult. The state has few major roads. The Kenai Peninsula, Valdez, and Fairbanks are all connected by a series of highways. But no roads lead to the state capital of Juneau. The only way to reach this city is by ship or by airplane.

Alaska's Ethnic Backgrounds

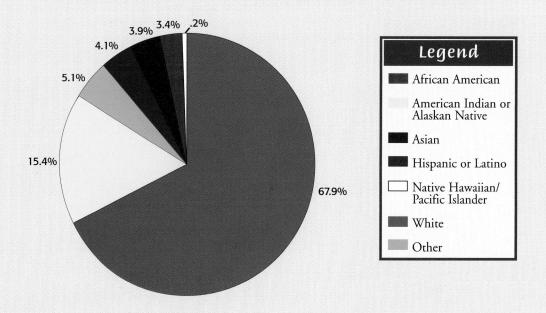

Legend
- African American
- American Indian or Alaskan Native
- Asian
- Hispanic or Latino
- Native Hawaiian/ Pacific Islander
- White
- Other

67.9%
15.4%
5.1%
4.1%
3.9%
3.4%
.2%

The backbone of Alaskan travel is the airplane. One in about every 50 Alaskans is a pilot. For many people, airplanes are the only way of getting in and out of mainland Alaska. Airplanes carry people, supplies, and mail throughout the state.

With Alaska's long coastline, ships are an important form of transportation. Many people use the Alaska Marine

Highway. This system of ferries carries passengers and cars from port to port in southern Alaska.

Art and Leisure

Music, theater, art, and dance are popular in Alaska. Anchorage has a symphony orchestra and the Anchorage Opera. Classical music lovers enjoy concerts from the Fairbanks Concert Association, the University of Alaska-Fairbanks music department, and the Juneau Symphony Orchestra. Juneau's Perseverance Theatre, the Fairbanks Drama Association, and

the Anchorage Repertory Theatre present a wide variety of plays each year.

Alaska has many museums. The Sheldon Jackson Museum, the Alaska Native Heritage Center, and the Anchorage Historical and Fine Arts Museum have collections of native treasures. The pen that signed the Alaska Statehood Act and the check for $7.2 million to purchase Alaska can be found in the Alaska State Museum at Juneau.

Native arts are a large part of Alaska's cultural life. Alaskan Natives produce ceramics, textiles, carvings, prints, and many

Ferries are an important part of Alaska's transportation system. Many cities along Alaska's coast are not connected by roads. People drive their cars onto ferries. The ferries carry them and their cars from city to city.

other handcrafted items. In the Tlingit Indian village of Saxman, native performers present their customs, history, myths, and songs at the Naa Kahidi Theater.

Sports

In general, Alaskans are athletic, outdoorsy people. Fishing, skiing, hiking, canoeing, snowshoeing, and ice skating are popular activities.

The state does not have any major league sports teams. But it does have its own amateur baseball league, the Alaska Baseball League. Ice hockey is a popular sport. Local teams

These Tlingit Indian dancers display their native customs in Saxman.

compete in leagues, and professional teams sometimes visit Alaska. Basketball is another popular sport in Alaska. At Thanksgiving, some of the best college basketball teams in the country compete in the Great Alaska Shootout in Anchorage's Sullivan Arena.

Dog mushing, or sled dog racing, is Alaska's official state sport. Alaskan Natives developed mushing as a way of traveling across snow. Today, dozens of sled dog races are held each year in Alaska. The most famous of these races is the Iditarod Trail Sled Dog Race.

Places to Visit

Alaska is full of historic sites and natural wonders. The Ketchikan area has the largest collection of totem poles in the world. In the Panhandle, people visit Wrangell. It is the only town in Alaska to have served under Russian, British, and U.S. flags. In Anchorage, visitors tour the 1915 Oscar Anderson House. This house was the city's first permanent wood-frame structure. In Fairbanks, people can visit a gold

Did you know...?
"Rondy" is short for
rendezvous. It is an occasion
for people to come together
and have fun. Several towns
in Alaska have an annual
rondy, featuring races,
games, sporting events, craft
exhibits, and food stands.
The Anchorage Fur Rondy is
held every February. It is one
of the largest winter
festivals in the country. The
Fur Rondy draws crowds
from all over the world.

camp or watch an old-fashioned saloon show. In Nome, people can pan for gold.

Alaska has many natural wonders. In Kobuk Valley National Park, visitors can tour two deserts, the Great Kobuk Sand Dunes and the Little Kobuk Sand Dunes. Passengers on Tanana River steamboats, near Fairbanks, can catch a glimpse of the wilderness as the pioneers saw it in the early 1900s. Visitors to the Denali National Park and Preserve can see grizzly bears, caribou, Dall sheep, foxes, and moose. At the Alaska Sealife Center in Seward, people can learn about the animals that live in Alaska's coastal waters.

Throughout its history, Alaska's untamed wilderness and riches have attracted adventurous people. Alaskans are proud of the mountains, glaciers, forests, and volcanoes that fill their state. They also are proud to make Alaska their home, turning what people once thought of as a frozen wasteland into one of the country's richest states.

Northern Lights

Alaska is one of the best places to see the northern lights. These brightly colored lights also are known as the aurora borealis. They sometimes can be seen in northern parts of the sky. The best time to see them is in winter.

The northern lights are created by electrically charged particles from the Sun entering Earth's atmosphere. The particles create displays of pale green and pink lights. Shades of red, yellow, green, blue, and violet lights also have been seen.

Native people have several legends about the northern lights. The Menominee believed the lights showed where the Manabai'wok could be found. These giants were the spirits of great hunters and fishers. Eskimos thought the lights were spirits of the animals they hunted. To some American Indians, the lights were the spirits of people.

Recipe: Blueberry Pie

Wild berries, such as Alaskan wild blueberries, grow throughout much of the state. You can use berries bought at a grocery store for this recipe.

Ingredients

4 cups (960 mL) fresh
  blueberries
¼ cup (60 mL) tapioca
1 cup (240 mL) sugar
1 tablespoon (15 mL) lemon
  juice
1 pie shell and crust
1 tablespoon (15 mL) butter or
  margarine

Equipment

dry-ingredient measuring
  cups
measuring spoons
medium mixing bowl
mixing spoons
nonstick cooking spray
9-inch (23-centimeter) pie
  pan
butter knife
pot holders
wire cooling rack

What You Do

1. Preheat oven to 400°F (200°C).

2. With a mixing spoon, mix blueberries, tapioca, sugar, and lemon juice in medium mixing bowl. Set pie mix aside for 15 minutes.

3. Spray inside of pie pan with nonstick cooking spray, then place pie shell in pie pan.

4. Pour pie mix into pie shell. Spread the pie mix evenly.

5. Place small pieces of the butter on top of the pie mix.

6. Place pie crust on top of the pie. Seal the edges of the crust. Cut several slits in the crust with the butter knife to permit steam to escape.

7. Bake 1 hour, or until juices form bubbles that burst slowly.

8. Let cool on a wire cooling rack before serving.

Makes 8 servings

Alaska's Flag and Seal

Alaska's State Flag

Alaska's state flag has eight gold stars on a field of blue. Seven of the stars are in the shape of the Big Dipper. This grouping of stars also is known as Ursa Major, or the great bear. The constellation represents Alaska's strength. The eighth star is the North Star. It represents Alaska's future and the state's position as the northernmost state.

Alaska's State Seal

Alaska's state seal shows a landscape. The building on the left is a smelter. It symbolizes the importance of mining to Alaska. A train in the picture stands for Alaska's railroads. Ships show the importance of transportation by sea. Trees symbolize Alaska's wealth of forests. A farmer in the foreground represents Alaska's agriculture. The fish and the seal along the state seal's outer edge show the importance of fishing and wildlife to Alaska's economy.

Almanac

General Facts

Nickname: The Last Frontier State

Population: 626,932 (U.S. Census 2000)
Population rank: 48th

Capital: Juneau

Largest cities: Anchorage, Juneau, Fairbanks, Sitka, Ketchikan

Agriculture

Agricultural products: Milk, poultry, eggs, beef, hay, potatoes

Climate

Hottest temperature: 100 degrees Fahrenheit (38 degrees Celsius), Fort Yukon, June 27, 1915

Coldest temperature: minus 80 degrees Fahrenheit (minus 62 degrees Celsius), Prospect Creek, January 23, 1971

Precipitation: up to 200 inches (508 centimeters)

Geography

Area: 615,230 square miles (1,593,446 square kilometers)
Size rank: 1st

Highest point: Mount Mckinley, or Denali, 20,320 feet (6,194 meters) above sea level

Lowest point: Pacific Ocean, sea level

Willow ptarmigan

Forget-me-not

Symbols

Animal: Moose

Bird: Willow ptarmigan

Fish: King salmon

Flower: Forget-me-not

Fossil: Wooly mammoth

Insect: Four spot skimmer dragonfly

Economy

Natural Resources: Oil, timber, natural gas, gold, zinc, coal, lead, silver

Types of Industry: Mining, fishing, logging, oil refining, food processing, tourism

Symbols

Marine mammal: Bowhead whale

Mineral: Gold

Motto: North to the future

Song: "Alaska's Flag," by Marie Drake

Sport: Dog mushing

Tree: Sitka spruce

Government

First governor: William Egan

Statehood: January 3, 1959 (49th state)

U.S. Representatives: 1

U.S. Senators: 2

U.S. electoral votes: 3

Organized boroughs: 16

Timeline

State History

1741
Vitus Bering sails
to Alaska.

1784
The first Russian
settlement in Alaska
is established on
Kodiak Island.

1880
Gold is discovered in
Alaska, setting off the
first of many gold rushes.

1867
U.S. Secretary of
State William
Seward buys Alaska
from Russia.

U.S. History

1775–1783
American colonists fight
for their freedom in the
Revolutionary War.

1812–1814
The United States and
Great Britain fight the
War of 1812.

1620
Pilgrims establish
a colony in the
New World.

1861–1865
The Civil War
is fought.

1912
Congress makes
Alaska a territory.

1977
The Trans-Alaska
Pipeline is completed.

1968
North America's largest known oil
field is found in Prudhoe Bay.

1989
The *Exxon Valdez*
hits a reef, spilling
oil into Prince
William Sound.

1959
On January 3, Alaska
becomes the 49th state.

1929–1939
The United States
suffers the Great
Depression.

1964
U.S. Congress passes
the Civil Rights
Act, which makes
discrimination illegal.

1914–1918
World War I is fought;
the United States
enters the war in 1917.

1939–1945
World War II is
fought; the United
States enters the
war in 1941.

2001
On September 11,
terrorists attack
the World Trade
Center and
the Pentagon.

Words to Know

diphtheria (dif-THIR-ee-uh)—a disease that causes a high fever, weakness, and difficulties in breathing

environmentalist (en-vye-ruhn-MEN-tuhl-ist)—a person who is concerned about nature

ethnic (ETH-nik)—having to do with a group of people who share similar national origins, language, and culture

frontier (fruhn-TIHR)—an undeveloped area where few people live

glacier (GLAY-shur)—a slow-moving sheet of ice found in mountains and polar regions

maritime (MA-ruh-time)—having to do with the sea

musher (MUHSH-ur)—the driver of a sled dog team

permafrost (PURM-uh-frawst)—ground that stays frozen year-round

prey (PRAY)—an animal hunted by other animals for food

reef (REEF)—a strip of rock, sand, or coral close to the water's surface

rendezvous (RON-day-voo)—a meeting at a certain time or place

tundra (TUHN-druh)—a frozen, treeless area

To Learn More

Feinstein, Stephen. *Alaska.* States. Berkeley Heights, N.J.: MyReportLinks.com Books, 2003.

Johnston, Joyce. *Alaska.* Hello U.S.A. Minneapolis: Lerner, 2002.

Kummer, Patricia K. *Alaska.* One Nation. Mankato, Minn.: Capstone Press, 2003.

Walsh Shepherd, Donna. *Alaska.* America the Beautiful. New York: Children's Press, 1999.

Internet Sites

Track down many sites about Alaska.
Visit the FACT HOUND at *http://www.facthound.com*

IT IS EASY! IT IS FUN!

1) Go to *http://www.facthound.com*
2) Type in: 0736815708
3) Click on "FETCH IT" and FACT HOUND will find several links hand-picked by our editors.

Relax and let our pal FACT HOUND do the research for you!

Places to Write and Visit

Alaska Native Heritage Center
8800 Heritage Center Drive
Anchorage, AK 99506

Glacier Bay National Park and Preserve
P.O. Box 140
Gustavus, AK 99826-0140

Juneau Convention & Visitors Bureau
One Sealaska Plaza
Suite 305
Juneau, AK 99801

Wickersham State Historic Site
House of Wickersham
213 7th Street
Juneau, AK 99801

This totem pole is one of many found at Saxman Totem Park in Ketchikan, Alaska. The park is known for having the largest collection of totem poles in the world.

Index

Chapter 5

West Union School
23870 NW West Union Road
Hillsboro, Oregon 97124